IF WE KNEW HOW TO WE WOULD

IF WE KNEW HOW TO WE WOULD

EMMA BARNES

First published 2025
Auckland University Press
Waipapa Taumata Rau
University of Auckland
Private Bag 92019
Auckland 1142
New Zealand
www.aucklanduniversitypress.co.nz

ISBN 978 1 77671 188 8

A catalogue record for this book
is available from the National
Library of New Zealand

Design by Kalee Jackson

This book was printed on
FSC® certified paper

Printed in China by 1010
Printing International Ltd

For all the ad hoc mental health support teams who are out there doing their best in an underfunded, seemingly unloving world.

This book deals with themes of suicide, grief and depression. It is important to me that you take care of yourselves when reading it. Please particularly avoid the middle section if you aren't up to this content.

'We don't see things as they are,
we see them as we are.'

— Anaïs Nin, *Seduction of the Minotaur*, p. 120

Contents

IN OUR HANDS

'Love doesn't just sit there, like a stone,
it has to be made, like bread;
remade all the time, made new.'

— Ursula K. Le Guin, *The Lathe of Heaven*, p. 159

Lineage

The man with the sharp knife cuts the fat to tissue paper thinness and two people fold it into their mouths: a sacrament, like frills, like folds. He returns to the carcass, cracks, and breaks a joint as an exclamation. His point made; his poetry recited; his lineage showing like marks on the skin. He is descended from Italian butchers back to time itself. He doesn't know it's ice cream, apples, and sheep for me. The gene for alcoholism hiding in plain sight, not even hiding if you think about it. The fat melts in my mouth on my tongue through my entire body as if it was able to travel on all my pathways. Warm and wet like a summer you never ordered. It leads me off course into a different timeline where the rules are so different I can't understand them. The shape of a forehead. The line of a jaw. The quick, unsubtle words you say to hold my shape to its current form. Let the butcher hold his knife. Let the butcher raise his pigs. Let the butcher slit my throat with intention and precision. I take it back. I'm not a pig in a field eating acorns and setting fat. I should have been. I could have been. The child of the children of farmers means nothing to me right now but it could have. I'll call out to be reborn with a squeal and a curly tail. Let me hold things solidly together. Let time reward my boldness. Let this little piggy cry all the way home. Eee, wee, wee, weee.

I asked

If we have to explain this to each other I want it to be known that I asked to be ground into dust. I asked to have my bones ground into bread. I asked with my mouth that no one can look at without thinking of kissing. I asked with the lips that have kissed a thousand mouths. I asked with the lips that kept you guessing that kept time alive in a different way. And when I asked I was polite. I used the correct register for the language we spoke in and I made sure all the parts of speech were as correct as they could be. I did my homework in the way of the traditional overachiever. I held your hand. I put my palm against your chest. I asked in all the right ways with all the different forms of request. I could be trusted. I followed all the procedures and policies that were laid out before me like a tapestry of compliance and then I followed them all. In the moments where I agree I may be autistic it is this type of situation that always confirms my belief. Please explain to me in detail what it is you require from me so I may meet every need. Then grind me into dust. Rub me between your fingers to make sure I'm just the right texture, the soft velvet of dust, enough. I want to be a powder for you. I want to be so smooth it's like I'm not quite there. I want to be brushed away. I want to be bashed out of a rug with a looping bamboo tool created for this exact purpose. I want you to know and see all of me in powder form. We were created for this exact purpose. We were created for you to tear me apart in a piece-by-piece fashion over a decade of love and arguments and never being quite right. We were created and then we were destroyed. It is the same story, repeated. It is the same set of feelings but in a slightly different package. It is everything, all at once.

Tensile strength

The tension exists in the muscles that run from my hands to my forearms to the webbed spread of musculature across my breastbone, my chest. Say the word muscle. I tell you. My face tilts. I am the tensile strength of muscle fibres through a stress-strain curve. A muscle can only pull. Even a push is a pull. Muscles pair for different directions and stresses. I am a full range of motion, exercised regularly. I lift at the intersection of my energies. The in and out and up and down and the back and forth. There are days where this is only anger, and it is like it is a hormone like it is the air around me. There are days where I'm so alive I'm suffused with blood and strength and focus. Then there are days where I am working it up with stolen energy, latent heat left behind from being in spaces. Before I experienced strength, I did not know this feeling of fullness, of possibility. I did not know about the way your energy can rise up through your body and leave through your head and move up into the higher layers of the atmosphere. I did not know I could be tired and so alive at the same time. I did not know that it would turn me into several different hungers. I did not know. But now I do it has not changed anything about me, or it has not changed anything sufficiently much, sufficiently enough to know much more than that. This was all one breath. Hissed out with a controlled core. I bounced at the top. That's how you know there's more.

The problem

The problem is that now I have taken you into my mouth I have taken you into my mouth. We're here. It's a day. It's amongst other days nested together. I don't really recall. I don't ever recall. It is too much to say nothing about. It is nothing to say too much about. We have been together. And I am unfortunate in my inability to not exist in that moment. But I also am not safe to be there. I shouldn't be allowed. I should be kept apart, at home, safe, wrapped in plastic. I turn into a script, a scroll, a set of prior instructions or commands. I just take it out, take it on, pull through. You are revealed slowly. And I'm in your lap. Or I'm against the lower half of your body. Or we're seeing how it feels for you to compress me into a single layer, a sheet. And then I have taken you into my mouth. You are a barrel. You are an extremely large set of shoulders. You are a man unconcerned with much because you are of a size to never have to care. I can't really imagine your reality though I'm impressed by it. I seek something in you. What it is I couldn't say. It is of no consequence. It does not matter. It is a leading indicator of nothing much. I am the problem. It is me. I can't be left alone. I can't be connected with a large man. I can't be let out of the house. I can't be. Just one large hand on my thigh and I'm cooked. Completely done. Ready to wet my lips with anticipation.

In your hands

We are standing in the deep dark of midnight. And your hands are there with me. I know that we are like gulfs, like gaps to each other. I know that there's a break we take together. It's walking as two bodies: our legs, in sync. It's that you are silence, and I am silence and together we are a loud sound, louder than we can really hear. We're all just noise eventually. You say you don't know, you don't love me, you don't crave anything but then you take me into a dark rectangle and pull me apart like I'm Meccano, like I'm soft bread in your fingers, like the sealed section of a *Cosmopolitan* in 1995: though you were barely alive. I am barely alive. Do I love you? What is love to midnight? What is love in a moment? What is a moment in any case. Love spread around like dust, held back like treasure, unexplained, unevenly distributed. Everyone I know just wants to be loved and is so afraid not to be met where they are. But I will meet you where you are for the joy of being where you are. Looking at you. Your hand on my throat like safety, like trust, like a promise of considered and careful behaviour driven by a complex understanding of consent. You are as afraid of me as I am unafraid of you, or the opposite. Whatever the division between us everything is revealed when I finally feel the strength in your hands. We are particles and wave forms, and we are localised or not and we are varied and misunderstood and aligned briefly through our curves. I grip your oblique muscles between my fingers as if they will steady me. You go quiet. I know you're there. Only you and I talk like this, in your life, you say. Then you laugh into whatever is happening now. We're all that's happening now. You say. You lean down for one more kiss.

Hold my hand

This man is small enough my hands reach right around him. This boy, this man, delighted on a street corner in the late dark of a moment before midnight. He knows so much and so little and so much and so little. I am the most tender holder of his safety. I am the person monitoring for the slack in the line and then the sudden tension. I have to tell you I absolutely have to tell you I wish I knew these things so much earlier. I wish that I knew of this great calmness inside me. This warm and tender heart that can live and live and live. What is it about the skin of some men where their throat and their neck meet? What is it about the gentle pressure of intention. What is it. I know when your eyes roll back in your head I will be watching you. I know. The shape you make as you fall back into it. We are all small enough to fit in pockets. We are small enough to be unseen. We are small enough to not see ourselves. We are small enough to skip and slip through cracks. And it is amazing that we are missed, that we remain unseen. But here we are hidden by that beautiful downy darkness together both beyond structuralist thought: boths and neithers and in-betweens and never said and hold my hand, hold my hand.

Damage

Who will do the damage in this exchange. I am the soft and older piece. You are the younger brittle section. I am the unquenchable tide. You are the repeatable trick. What if none of us do anything? What if we suspend all romance for the foreseeable future and instead return to the inert state of pre-beginning. Why is romance a small word to explain ten thousand other things you never knew were part of this. I hear all your unsaid nos and pivot in front of them and around them and away from them and into new directions you might find more appealing. I want so much more than I ever let myself have. Please connect up the cables of my existence in the safest manner as if you know that there should be no need for a connection that sets this all afire or stops any one heart in the service of another. I don't understand electricity enough to follow you but it all comes down to the diagram and who drew it and how it flows. The apples shake the tree. The stars send light through years. I worry at the unexplained pain of my insides. I am now too aware of everything. The passage of time is everything around me moving in a different direction. Pick up the pick-up sticks. We stand on this street, together, holding hands.

I am a circle

I am a circle, completing myself. The sunshine rings like a note from your throat. You laugh. You drain the sky of all colour as if it is simple, nothing, an afterthought. We are empty in the empty streets but we're only empty because there's room to move. The steps are I touch you and you touch me and then I touch you again but differently. A first touch might be your fingers on my chin. Or my hand curling around a neck. Every person who has kissed me recently has said: can I kiss you? Every kiss has shifted against itself like a body rolling over in bed. In the low light I can't tell your eyes are amber, but I know they are. I am not sorry to tell you I've been reaching higher during the day. Reaching up and up. Feeling my body become a tower as I go to *pointe* as I feel my ligaments lengthen. I reach up there to the cooler temperatures to the thinner atmosphere to the eventual space I find for myself. That space is not uncomplicated. I am not uncomplicated. You especially are not uncomplicated. You can see I'm made of fibre, of the woven rope of hair my mother kept in a box on the top shelf of her closet. You can see I'm one thousand years old in a body made of the decisions of ancestors and the cold crush of time. You can see something there. A reflection. A mirror made of dust and the differences between us. I don't know what you see. I only know you see it. And it is in the way you kiss me. It is in the patience I don't even have to cultivate. My body and I care less and less about being an understandable shape when we are touched and held and cared for. You can fuck softness too. And I am not only softness. I can't remake your ideas about my body, but I can remake my own. I can remake myself over and over until I am here after midnight on a Thursday with my fingers a curve on your neck, my thumb a splint, my lips against yours, not even a person anymore, a thing. All things are possible, all things are counted and made and rebirthed and let out into the night.

A series of gates

You might be unknown to me. You say things out loud. You kiss me back. My mind will not believe you willingly – *I come to a gate. I get off the horse. I open the gate. I lead the horse through the gate. I close the gate. I get back on the horse* – I imagine we could be a door marked push and a door marked pull and we could have discussions about the interplay between us. In my mind I can see us as a bridge being built from different sides of the same river. I think we will align. I can see a time where I just look into you and you look into me as we build something else together – *I come to another gate. I get off the horse. I open the gate. I lead the horse through the gate. I close the gate. I get back on the horse* – I will be patient and willing to learn. I might even let you teach me. I might even let you place your fingers around my throat to rest there. The spread of your palm across the most nervous part of my form. No tension. No pressure. Just resting. Offering you a pulse. Letting you feel my breath. What will we say to each other. I will close my eyes and still be able to see you. The absolute tenderness of your eyes. The hesitance of your mouth – *I come to another gate. I get off the horse. I open the gate. I lead the horse through the gate. I close the gate. I get back on the horse* – You return like a tide. You have a kind of gentle reserve. But then you say something direct. The moon turns around to watch us. Somehow here on the same empty street. Who started this particular meeting of mouths? I have to stand on the tips of my toes to reach you. To reach you I grow outside myself. I am taller than the sky. I know all the trees' names – *I come to another gate. You open the gate. You lead the horse through the gate. You close the gate and look up into my eyes.*

The core

I have looked into your eyes so many times and yet this time the feeling is a soft and open field, a bed covered in white pristine bedding. You are so tenderly expectant of nothing but seem hopeful for more. The kisses are like pastels and they are in the sunlight, bright sunlight. We are usually in darkness together where all edges are rubbed to fuzz. But how sweet is this sunlight, to be so revealed, an excavation by radiance. A river washing us free of debris, of nighttime, of any uncertainty. Your fingers find a way to slip through mine and our bodies lean into each other without either of us telling them to do so. It's the day you tell me you have fallen in love with me in the most casual way I've ever heard it. In the moment my body went through the floor without me and journeyed down through the hot centre of the earth while the rest of me was suspended across the table from you as you ate, the cheese course. My mouth, shocked into silence by arriving at the core of the matter, the core of the earth, beneath the mantle. The flush of heat replicated from cell to cell to cell to cell. Somehow still living we carry on through my surprise and your calm and casual statements. To my surprise you do exist and I can touch you and your mouth is a welcome and my hand on your belly is real and true and I can look up into your face like it is also the sun, like we are all light, like every moment of this is the sunrise and the day is ahead of us, the day is yet to come, the day is starting with so much light.

The compass and the horse

I go forward one step. I step to the side then backwards three steps. I find all my dials and instruments running in circles like a compass with too much metal in the earth, too many electrical fields. I deviate. I go haywire. I act against my own wishes. All because of your softly ageing skin and the sound of your laugh. Are you just a performance? Am I just a nervous system reaction? How does this keep happening to me. I walk past you and realise it wasn't me you loved. The brain won't hold the current state. It reverts with a simple and small trigger. Back eight years in time. Some of me crawling into the now where I can hold my own against the thoughts that made me. It was a different time I say to myself in a low careful voice. I was a different person I say to no one in particular in the same gentle tone. I talk to myself like I'm a horse taken to panic. Stroke the flanks. Breathe the air. Calm the farm. Did you remember to be as calm if not calmer than the horse. Does the horse remember anything. Are you the horse? Am I the horse too? Are we both horses galloping at speed through space? I know several things I never used to. I know several orders of magnitude more than that. But I've been knowing nothing forever. Just a little pattern of nothing. Repeated. Both these states are true. Both these states are you. I hold myself up in a state of in-betweenness. Spine at stretch. Full height in centimetres is only one hundred and sixty-one. It's not that much. It's nothing. Back to the start. I go forward one step.

To knit is to code is to code is to knit

How many times. Too many times. This many times. A person has pinned another person down to a single moment. I will say it is understandable. To want to make it simple. It is a simple thing to want it to be without pain. To be without pain or to know that there could be truth. Truth is an idea. It fails to accommodate circumstance. We hurt and unwind each other like spools of thread tangling, left dangling, left twisted. Unspooling into water. Rolling down hills. Twisting and interleaving, weaving. Fraying and breaking, a snap or the grinding of shears cutting in two. To knit is to code it back together, back to language. A sequence that forgives the tension in the hand, or not, as it happens. Gaps and holes turn into a garment so half of it is space. Half of it is thread. A coil of French knitting, like intestines. A tidy fan of lace. Messy and worn in awareness of absences. *I know I hurt you.* I am aware of the gaps within myself. I leave a little bit of openness for a future though I knit around you, I knit around us. I knit into a future world where thread and gap combine to wrap our history, neatly or lopsided. The gaps that made us then are not the gaps that make us now.

Famous knots of history

I am knots and fighting. Wound into circles that don't make sense. We're all skin at some point. Attraction is a knife blade of separation. But shouldn't it be different under love. I never thought of myself as anything to desire until I did. Now I am attached to it and its absence pulls like a sucking swamp and drags me back through time to a loneliness so intense I don't know how to think my way out of out of it. How would you know anything about this. I flicker like I'm a hologram. I manage to look at enough sea that it becomes me. I wish I could turn my body into successive rays of light so I would never have to feel this feeling of feelings piled up going backwards into the earth like a rut. I challenge myself to be gentle to be smaller to be different to let it float like a message written in the sky but I am of the earth I am dirt I am the loam of trees and disease. I am unease made flesh. I am ringing a bell. Then you are a tender wall. A gentle building. A soft bridge. The most velveteen wrecking ball. I am replaying the same VCR in a dark room pretending this is where I live. You rest your chin on my shoulder as we watch the sun enter the sea. You will leave me. I will be left but I will be different than when you found me. I rethread the needle. I unspool the threads. I stitch.

Choke

I don't have much more to say on this subject. I have cashed out my shares and along with it my responsibility to tell a tale in a sane and logical manner so we're here at the dregs. We're here in the final minute where no one makes sense and everyone feels something they didn't think they'd feel in a space they didn't know they'd feel it in. I meet a man who can put you to sleep in the tight embrace of his arms. Remains to be seen if this is a trick of the light, a problem or just something some people learn to do for fun. I think about him holding me. I think about him letting the unfinal darkness in. I think about him letting in the final darkness. This is what we're here to talk about. Those minutes where maybe you do or do not know about the finality. I sometimes make a list of what I think the final thoughts might be. Will it be a running list of hands that have loved me? Or will it be a distracted grasp at wanting more? What faces could appear? How much is that minute in brain time? How many thoughts can you fit into a clown car. It all remains to be seen but I like to head up to the edge and retreat again. I like to be around and around and around on this one. Just imagine me as a small bird getting into your nectar. Just imagine me as the tide, always, always returning and somehow always, always leaving. You didn't make it clear enough at any point and so I've just imagined the rest. That's how it goes around here. Gaps are filled. Lines are written. Time is turned into something else so that when we're there when we're at the very end we probably won't know it. There's so much I don't want to find out. There's so much I just want to leave here, leave behind, leave alone. Don't turn the stone over. Don't ask the question, yet.

Skinful

A handful of blood. A mouthful of spit. A neckful. A skinful. Full of something. Stretched taut. The taste of you. The two words we know. That moment I can never describe where you slide through me like you're looking to find something in me that doesn't exist. Or something in me only you know exists. It could be either. I will never tell or know the difference. I am never told and I never know the difference. I spend half the afternoon imagining our faces close together. I remember it as I'm half out of my body. It's a feeling being tweezed from between layers of skin like a splinter. Two bodies leaning in close. I know when you come through the bubble of space around me. I feel all the hairs on my body stand on end. I monitor for incursions. I monitor edges. I am a learned border. I broadcast no. You make it through and leave again. This step repeats. I find the no eventually gets turned down. Who makes it through the broadcast. Only those who cannot hear it? Those who hear it and disregard it? Those who know what it means? What do you think it means? What do I think it means. Where does no come from. A skinful of no. A mouthful of no. A handful of no. I am five cups full of the knowledge of refusal. I am baking a very large cake that says rejection to anyone who puts it in their mouth. I reject everyone who takes me into their mouth. Or anyone I take into my mouth. Rejection is all around us. I go first.

Chain of connected resentment

It is the unbelievable mess. It is the sweeping leaking sign of the times. It is all of it. I would like to collect the fee for an exorcism or some sort of ritual clearing of the air. I would like to hold hands and reset the night into something new. But here we are. All of us holding hands in one big chain of connected resentment. I know how you speak about me when I'm not in the room and I try so hard not to be the same way. My words I try to align like a compass to the north star. I know you I know you I know you but I also know that there are always gaps and circumstances and reasons and we're all just dust eventually why would we spend any time being unkind to each other on purpose. I slid my fingers inside you many times. I rested my mouth against your lips over and over. I was the grumpiest person you knew. Why could we never just talk. Why could we never just hold each other. Why is there always so much in the way. This other woman I loved and I miss. This other woman who scooped out parts of me like a melon baller. Like a finger dragged through a pudding, through onion dip. The other woman. The list is long enough without you. I feel like we are always learning something and somehow never ever learning anything. Perched on the edge of self-actualisation. Perched on the edge of real true discovery about someone, some thing, ourselves. Only to turn back at the last minute in search of what? I will tell the young people my secrets. I will tell the even slightly middle-aged my secrets. I will tell a bunch of people a bunch of things. I'll tell you nothing. I lie. Come back. I'll tell you. I want you. I'll tell you. I never stopped. I hate that love for you resides inside me. I know love is there forever once it starts. Just on simmer. Wasting energy. Going and going and going.

Mistakes in disambiguation

In this we are the same. In this we are different. In this we reach an accord after months of debate only to find out that we've actually disagreed on a central point due to a misunderstanding via terminology we should have disambiguated. These are the risks we take. The way that words don't mean anything together and sometimes they mean more apart. I would have said before now that I was incapable of making you out to be anything but the bad guy. And I find that the bad guy role is one that's too simple, too flat. Too easy to fit you into in a way that ignores so much about you and more about me. Not the bad guy, the terrible couple, the awful twosome, the maddest match in town. We were out of our minds and we were just untethered from reality in a way that means we were looking down upon ourselves and still somehow choosing to condone this behaviour. The first time we kissed you told me to slow down and I have slowed so much since that I've become glacial. I picked up the pace once or twice and immediately regretted it. I have reset the internal clock to run at a pace that's almost never matched. One time, one time it was. These days I push against the flat of the chest to hold it all back. The world held back by its breastbone. The need inspired by circumstance ignored by the next set of circumstances. You're a lily pad. I'm a wax figurine. We're all transformed by lust into something madder than we were before. We're all transformed into our little horny cries. That one final breath you expel before understanding exactly what happened to you. I am somehow shorter all the time and in reaching up I am more than reaching up. But with you we were mouths at the same height. No stretching, no bending. Always there. Lips ready. Heart barely intact. But lips always at the ready for a kiss too tender to speak of for a name that can't say itself. The time unwound and went back to front before I noticed anything. And here I am saying nothing to myself in the cold hard night. I was alone before I met you and alone while I was with you and here I stand on this cold beach in a state of divine intervention and you could say so much more than you'd ever, than you ever managed to. I was given a set of ears but I have up until this point refused to use them, on you.

The dry middle

The blankest part of the story hangs around. The dry middle. The part just before we get anywhere. We're stuck here. Repeating lessons because we haven't learned them yet. We haven't learned much. I haven't learned much. I should say. I hold myself apart. But that's not the move here. I hold myself back. And again. You gotta move forward and move in. The wind makes the windows clack. The sound of the outside comes in. I couldn't have imagined this much time passing. I thought we were safe in the huddle of a small number of years but of course that would end. Of course it would extend outwards and thin out. Of course. I would reach an age I wouldn't understand and be set adrift into it. It's not that I don't understand it's that I can't comprehend being the age I am. The age around me is generally incomprehensible but still I get it, I get it. But how is it possible I am this age. This age. And how is it possible some things didn't work. I don't know how to atone or if I even should. I am not sure what was broken or if I could fix it. I just know there's this part of me yearning, for you. How did I get here. Why do I retain the exact shape of your neck. We are the shapes the world made us. We are the longer stories cut short. We are the feet who walked us here.

Don't worry, baby

I see you and I see you and I see you. You collect up like drifts like small piles of wind-driven trash. In corners with your head purposefully not making eye contact and I care but not in the caring way. I care for all the past versions of selves that I wrecked on the shores of your complete inability to articulate a single need, a single desire, any sort of boundary any one human might understand. When we hug it's still the universe clanging together. And if I had to label love your name would be close to the top of the list. But here it is. You just a shadow. Me a complete self. Don't make me say it. Don't let them hear it. Don't worry, baby. Our time is gone. And I only sometimes trick myself into a future recollection that says somewhere, somehow, sometimes we're all together and the sun will be shining and you'll laugh and take my hand. This is not a recommended future. This is only the smallest fantasy about to be squeezed through the eye of a needle. My complete fortune going begging. Spilled into the sunshine like glass or a spray of light. Like the wounded howling of a bull dissatisfied. Like the memory of a dance the night before. These vibes conflict but there is a kind of harmony to all this. To the way I narrowly avoided destroying the entire universe. If only we'd known at the beginning. If only we'd known at all.

IF WE

KNEW

HOW TO

WE

WOULD

PYLADES: I'll take care of you.
ORESTES: It's rotten work.
PYLADES: Not to me. Not if it's you.

— Excerpt from 'Orestes by Euripides' from *An Oresteia*, translated by Anne Carson, p. 218

The squeeze

The grief squeezes up on you. A tight constriction of feeling and breathing. What leaves and doesn't come back. What leaves that you know is gone but aren't ready to say out loud. Now is haunted by later. Later rides up in a van and slides the door open to grab you off the street. Your feet don't touch the earth. Some connections sever. The Wi-Fi restarts without you. The lights flash into the mid-dark of dusk. You're your own ghost now. See through. Seeing it through. A flyover of the city on your own power. Lost up in the night like several hundred birds, each wing flap a different heartbeat. Don't question whether ghosts have hearts. They have ten thousand. They have none. It's all the same. Both and neither is the way everything is all at once. Shedding tears backwards through time. Leaving a damp trail for myself to get back to where everything started, to stop it. Every Sunday is a slap in the face. The sting lingers. The sting of fingers. We are just a moment. Just one small moment. Happening forever.

Astigmatism

Is it the way light flares around its source in the night that makes me like this? The shapes of my eyes, irregular. The reaction to blur, to ache, to lack focus. But it's the night and the fractured light that lead me to reckless romanticism. I will always hope somewhere to not be addressed as if I were simply a body to be used and discarded. As if for some reason in some moment I was without my self and would be subject to your reduction. But here we are with you saying this and my heart beating through it all. There are gaps in understanding and then there are gaps in understanding. In a not-dark nighttime I look into his face and feel the love between us like the spectrum flaring around a street light. It shifts in circles. I look away and look back my entire existence struggling through weariness. This time in our lives is filled with dragging mud. It's filled with auras around lights around the small acts of everydayness we continue with. I continue, somehow. I am continuing. I am tender. I am tender and I find my hand to be the right size to hold things. And I hold things without a second thought where I previously would have failed to grip, or not seen or something, something else. The tendons pull tight into a curl around you.

Promise

I feel all of this in my arms. It's the awareness of my bones floating in my flesh or the fatigue in my muscles or a simple shooting pain. I feel all of this. In this room with all of these people and my body tired from pulling things off the ground. The layers to speech and rooms and people. I withdraw with the threads. I sew myself shut. Will there be generosity from anyone in this space. Is everything I do wrong. How do I make myself into something that can be here. I can't control the image. I am beyond its edge. The edge is where we meet. The same edge where you want me to promise I won't take my own life. A heavy blanket drops onto my body and flattens me beside you as I think of the many times I have tried not to exist while still somehow trying to exist. You cannot ask anything more of me than trying. I know the looping interior of a brain convinced dying is living is saving is freedom is an end to the feeling upon feeling upon feeling is the next correct course of action. You introduce me to a drunk man who tells me he knows me from Tinder, I'm too impressive to swipe right on. Then you introduce me to a man who could not give a fuck. And then I am introduced for the third time to a man who says maybe my name will stick as if he is doing me a favour by seeing me as a person, even though he does not see me as a person. Every woman I'm introduced to takes me in, takes me right in. I am unknown and unknowable even to myself. But I won't promise to not take my life. I can't promise not to take my life. It's not reasonable to ask me not to take my life. It's not love. It's not possible. It's just something safe for you at this moment. It's just a few words but I only have words. And I only have the knowledge that now isn't forever and it works both ways. I won't always feel like this. But I won't always feel like this.

Without root

I cut off all ties. Let the light go. Let it all fall off into some kind of backdrop. Crack my own egg. You know. What is the sound of this going well. What is the shape of this going better than expected. What is it all, at all. You know that I have long forgotten whatever it was I wish I remembered. And I have said over and over that this cannot be as good as it gets. This cannot be as far as it goes. This won't be it. Unless it is. In which case here we are. Here we are. If I could manifest anything in this moment it would be someone walking up to me and taking hold of me like they knew I really wanted to be recognised. They should just do it, that's what. It should just happen. And that's the first and most important thought. It's the first and most important action. I believe that they can't see two feet in front of their nose. I believe they don't know what's happening around them. The old stories are powerful. The old names and words and times and things. I do wish there were as many ways in as there were ways out. I wish there were sidelines and alleyways and paths I've never stepped on or something like that. Something like you. Something like the way it was a thing that happened. The way it was a time we knew. The way it was an evidence-based policy that informed our future actions and needs and desires and wants and words. None of this makes sense. It is ten years since you told me to slow down and I think you'll find I'm still going way too fast. But you are not the fucking boss of me. I want to scoop out my insides with a melon baller, or some other device that makes this possible. Ten years is too long to be living like this. A decade. It's a type of journey. It's one thing or another. It's nothing to me any longer which is a lie the moment I say it but here we are and there we were. There we were. We didn't learn anything.

On the day I found out you killed yourself

In a single second it is done. It just happens between one and another. I don't believe it. I could never believe it. I could've never believed it. I didn't have it in me to believe it. Believing it wasn't possible. I didn't have the belief inside me. I didn't have the belief outside me for that matter. I cannot believe it. I won't believe it. I haven't believed it for a second. I will not believe it. I haven't considered for a second the idea of believing it. I won't entertain the thought. The thought will never cross my mind. Believing is not an option. I am incapable of believing. I am not made to believe. Belief is not in my vocabulary. Belief is not in my DNA. Belief, never heard of her. I don't even know how to spell it. Belief. Believed. Crack me open like a fucking egg and there's nothing inside, I swear it. I'm the great absence of belief. I am locked into this plan now. I have committed. No belief ever. I won't hold the centre. I can't be contained by this thing, this idea, this fact. This is an absence of fact zone. No one else is allowed to believe here either. No entry with a belief. The belief-sniffing dogs will meet you at the door. The door will meet your ass on the way out if we catch a whiff of it. The door will hit your ass on the way out. The way out comes but once. And once it comes you'll know it. And I still won't be believing it. My brain will just reject the thought over and over. No connection allowed. Connection rejected. Send the word away. The word never belonged here in the first place and we will remind it of that fact at every single opportunity from now until the end. Send it away. Send it further away. It is not possible. No.

Albatross

I have crashed into the ground like an albatross landing. My body is a bruise. My heart, capable of nothing. My breath sucked out through my mouth, my lungs, the space between my throat and my chest. It is a slap to the surface. It is a breach of trust. It is a gap in understanding. It is a ride, a ride, a ride. I repeat things when I am upset. She died. She died. She died. How do you say that more clearly? She died. I didn't say it out loud. I didn't appear at the moment she needed me. I had no knowledge of what was going on. I was in the dark. I was separate. I was alone, no hand on my thigh. There was no other body in the space for me to read electrical currents from. It was as if a great silence descended the moment it happened. The life leaving her body mirrored the way everything else left me. We leave each other in the moments we most need each other. You say this like it is the truth. Like there is a truth. Like there is anything. There's nothing. She died. What is it to end. She ended. Like drawing closer to the edge of a black hole all time felt as if it was suspended. My own event horizon. I invent five more feelings in this everlasting minute and call it even. How do I touch you after being in this space here where I cannot touch her ever again. It is a smallness that is unspeakable, yet it speaks.

The seams of time

You know that you have seen all of this leaking through the seams of time. I want you to adjust to and know that this could have been prevented. That this was all just a shot a shot in the unforeseeable future. The things I say are inevitable. The timing is obscure. The reach. The back channel. The cow bell. I was only a drummer for five minutes but what a five minutes. It was five minutes. Back to back. I found controlling arms and legs at once to be so intense it rewired me. I came back with new firmware and found rhythm in the rhythm. There were more layers to go. There were more words to say. There was a lot more to be revealed at a secret location, later. I can tell you the first place the second place the third place. No one counts past three. Some people count to five. Others can go higher and higher and higher. But we don't need to set a limit here. We can go on into the night. Into the next pairing. Into the sharp relief of daylight. Or later when someone reaches out to touch you and say: you seem attractive. You *seem* attractive. The large man in the sauna just actually looks like a slab of beef. He is so huge from far away and beside you he is overwhelming. You are overwhelmed and just trying to get some water at the same time. Who knows how those two things go together usually but here we are and here they are and here we are together. Overwhelmed and hydrated we face all the separate days that eventually will have run together. You don't say something to me every day and now I react to you with a feeling similar to anger that I shut down in every moment in order to continue on faithfully with you but still it rests there like anger like a feeling of anger like the first step in my brain shutting down because it is at tolerance at tolerance at the end of its rope. I don't usually say the word rope. It is an incitement. I am a clean slate with no acknowledgement of any messy reality. I don't want to say the word because the word is too powerful on its own. The word holds too much meaning and too much weight and there are just too many other words we could be saying at the same time. But I am now defaulting to not saying words. I am wordless. I don't know how to say a word. I will simply not say a word. I've already said too much. My anger blocks me from any other feeling. But here I am and here I am and here I am. With a future voice capping my throat. You have known what this means. I have known what this means. Our lives are held in the palms of people who don't care about us. And there it is. The truth of the matter not held back. Just set free. I know the secret to the universe and the universe knows me. I am too old for this shit. 43,000 years have passed. Take me back in time to where my neck doesn't have a wattle like a bird. I used to be made of sunlight of the sound of youth crashing on the shore. Someone who hates me walked past me and the sheer power of their dislike lifted my head so I looked straight into their eyes. We are all full of more meaning than any of us will admit to.

The word

The word will rise up out of the earth like it is an oak growing like it is a mine shaft being ejected like it is a mountain in the making. It will be so large and so overpowering that we will have to stop in the street to let it have its way. And its way will be had. This word the word of all words. The alpha the omega. But no god. No master. No overpowering prudish dogma to be had in this state, in this place, in this cleaving, in this cove. The word. The word of all words. The word to end further words. The word. I could say it. But I would feel like cutting my tongue out afterwards. I would feel like never speaking again. I would feel like so many disparate things trying to look cohesive in a coat made from worsted wool for twentieth-century soldiers. I am sure I would. The word might just rip me apart. I might attempt to rip the word apart. Either way something is getting destroyed tonight. The small weak sounds I make on seeing anything like the word in front of me. The way I don't even know myself in this place when the word is there. You could look and you could judge and you could tell me your judgement and what would it be. It would be something along the lines of weak in the knees at the presence of the word. The word. I have said the word and instantly regretted it. I have not said the word and instantly regretted it. News you can use. The word arrived. The word evolved. The word pinned me to the floor, to the collector's case, to the bed, like any number of people and things. I want you to know I notice you. The word notices you. The word comes clean in the dark after the lights are off. Turn the lights off, the word wants to kiss in the dark.

To them

It rises out of you. It is a vapour, a cough, a shine to your skin. You, unaware, unknowing, under a different impression don't see the signs. You don't see. And the signs won't see you. It's a good joke that neither side sees the other. In the middle is there nothing or something? This week we found out you died. This week we had several opportunities to speak your name in rooms. This week we held hands, this week we touched quietly in a hallway, this week we embraced on the street. After this week was over there was somehow another week and then another week. We still exist. I can't explain it. I walk through a lot of different doors, some of them I pull, some I push. Many of them slide open before me like curtains, like that art installation I saw in Berlin where a set of doors on a wall opened for anyone approaching and closed silently as they left. This metaphor is too heavy handed. Yes, ok, no one could walk through them. Berlin was unwelcoming. The bike couriers yelled too much and too loud and the past just sat around smoking cigarettes in the street, looking at you, winking if you noticed it. I attempted to be friendly to myself in the absence of others who were willing to do so. But even then leaving was a relief. You can struggle for so long and then you can still just succumb. A cruelness. A cruelty. A true unfairness. Would it have made a difference to hear your name spoken this much? I suspect it wouldn't have. You left and it wasn't a relief. You left and it was a spreading sickness amongst us. A terrible grief until someone sent you up to the stars. But they sent you to the stars. You were sent to the stars. I speak your name out loud most days. Most days I say your name.

If we knew how to stay alive we would

I am on the beach looking for you.   From the beach I can see her rising.
On the beach on the beach on the.   She is lifting up from the edge of it.
My heart is trapped in a sea shell.   I lift it to my ear and hear my blood.
My blood back and forth and back.   She is covered in red like blood like.
Have I shattered my small eardrum?   The phone rings and rings and rings.
You have to at some point close the   loop of adrenaline response by crying.
I tune in to the echo of her wish.   It is all instinct then it is not it is not.
I have not done the thing I said   I would do but I did do something else.
On the beach in the cold dark.   A kilometre seems a lot smaller now.

Later on when I am wedged into her side my face damp with tears and sweat she holds me like a giant mother, not the mother of giants but a mother giant enough to finally make me feel small enough to be held like this as the world spins out in front of me all at once and never again and all at once still, still.

It goes up and down and up again   then it's down very down, down low
and I have been there but it is like   when you leave it you can't remember
the way out. The birds ate all my   fucking breadcrumbs and I can't think
clearly enough to offer anything   useful except the small and now pallid
phrases of I love you. What a   poor tent peg, what a too small anchor.
How is anyone supposed to keep   doing anything under these conditions.
But then we are continuing. The   roots of your hair grow dark. The winter
has somehow mostly passed for   now even if it still continues to rain and
rain. Even if everyone is still   somehow, sick. We are all so very sick.

I spent twenty minutes in the rain today shovelling moss off concrete. It was trying to make dirt and it was succeeding. It slid up and off like the skin on warm milk and I was comforted by the smell of dirt, the inevitability of rain and the small act of labour. My palms felt a little worn afterwards. Worn back to nothing, to bone. Worn from a different labour, the labour of birthing something else. I am worn from the labour of birthing your sense of hope. If we knew how to stay alive we would.

The project

Internally, I talk you off a ledge. Internally, I talk myself onto the same ledge so we have the same perspective. I talk myself back out again, for safety. Internally, or externally, I have a side pony like it's the eighties as we have this discussion about the benefits of believing in the ability of any of us to continue existing. I go to a course that asks me to relearn hope and to share hope and to encourage hope and to be the hope you don't have in this world, today. But I don't have hope for the hope I'm supposed to generate from nothing like I'm an alchemist or some type of cosmic dust causing an explosion. Snap fingers into existence. Snap fingers into a click of thunder reminiscent of Zeus. Tonight, Matthew, I'm going to be a vague sense of my own ability to continue onward through the confusing ethical dilemma of how long you should sustain, as a project, trying to keep someone else alive. What's the answer. What's the answer. No one is prepared to talk to me about this. The only message is hope. I lifted a 7-foot-tall body off the ground and carried it home in my palm like a little bug. Will you talk to me about it now? Will you talk to me about it? Will you open that mouth to say any single word on the topic? I would have regretted dying had I made it come true for myself. So I continue onward as if it's the same truth for others repeated. But I don't know any answers. I don't know any cosmic truth. It's all ones and zeroes and ones again. And it might as well be Morse code or Latin or any other language I barely understand (all of them). All these people just pretending! Did you know so much was pretend? Did you know so much was contingent, simply hinged on a lie we all don't even tell ourselves, we just know to be 'true'? I departed from the common understanding of day to day in May 2022. Left the world for another realm. Didn't return. It wasn't up to me. Staying over night after night where I've been invited but haven't wanted to be.

Flow

I reach out through light years and you know that time is wrapping around you like a cloak, like an arm you know and love. Time zipping around like it doesn't have to make sense. Time resting on your shoulders on its own time on the minutes and hours we eat through together bite after bite after bite after bite. I know that you have been here. I know that time has collected on your eyelashes like snowflakes. I know that you know that you know things you wouldn't necessarily admit out loud. There are men with too much chin. There are men with too little chin. There are men with a perfectly average amount of chin who just pass through their days not even knowing they're in the middle of a bell curve. What do you think about your own chin. Is it like looking into a mirror and not being able to see your face or is it something more complex, less complex, easier to understand under pressure under duress under a timer. And back we are to the beginning to the first concept that just collects and builds up and runs across everything. What are first principles when it comes to time. What are the rules. How do you say the rules. How do you know the effect. How do you know anything else that might be related but isn't specifically named as a party to this venture. Don't make me tell you. I will say nothing with this mouth. I will say nothing with these veins and this blood and the heavy thickness of muscle that will gently roll in your hand. My time is short and the words might flow or the words might not flow or maybe they have already flowed or maybe you don't even know when the lights are on or the lights are off or the lights were never mentioned or you have held you hand over the bulb to be able to get a brief reprieve from the glare of what may as well be a sun. I will tell you. I will form those sentences with my mouth with the speed of light with the echoes of time with it all with it all. Maybe I will. Maybe I won't. If I said I would did I have to mean it? I didn't I didn't I didn't. I will regret things later when I'm dead, when I'm you, when I'm nothing like I've ever been ever before. There's no time to regret like now. There's no regret like I've ever said and seen and felt. There's nothing you could say to make me change my mind and there's simply just a quick little wish held between hands, held between fingers, held in breath and breaths and breaths and would you know if I hadn't said it? What exactly would you know?

Gaps

If I could spell it out I would. But it's not a thing that's capable of being words. If I could do anything about anything about anything I would but I am not capable of doing anything about anything about anything. I won't look. I won't listen. I won't arrange my atoms in a more acceptable fashion. I won't be quiet. I won't say anything. I won't let you know I have any feelings at all. I won't even know if you touch me. I won't even know if you look at me. I won't even know. I am just a big clean absence of anything. I could be a void but even that's got too much going on I'm way more nothing than that. I'm just so much nothing I've never seen this much nothing at once. How do you talk about the gap where something should be but instead it's just nothing. How do you signal to the crowd? How do you how do you how do you? The answer is you can't, you don't, you won't. It's not possible. I don't need to know what is possible. I don't need to know what's not. There's nothing I really ever need to know. I can be a total absence of knowing, of being, of seeing, of doing, of speaking. I am everything without you and nothing with you and it's almost like you never knew that. Hyperbole is the purview of the spurned. Hyperbole is the realm of the unfairly maligned. I am alive, alive. I'm alive. I'm not going to say anything. I'm the gap that will not speak its own name. I won't open my mouth. I can't be forced into it or forced out of anything.

Like a prism

I, too, am like a prism. Nothing to see here. But something to see here. Wait until the light hits my friend. Then we'll see. And what do we see? One angle. One thin layer. One sheet. One, one, one. Perhaps more. But how many pages in this book. How many sheets to a ream. In this dream we are all able to be our full selves. In this story all sides are covered and considered. We are all able to be amicable and have the hard discussion easily. We know the spots we struggle to see about ourselves. We say the things to each other in a way so gentle, small birds land on our outstretched fingers. I am an image of myself experiencing myself subjectively. Just like that song. Just like another song. Just like it. I walk along the harbour's edge internally screaming. It's joy this time though. You wouldn't know it, necessarily. But from here I'm able to see an old version of the city and an old version of the sea. An old version of me. And to this knowledge, to my knowledge, to the collective knowledge of history spread out across waves and wood and sunlight reflected this is a good place to be landing in. The jellies are billowing around the salted ocean. The sun is apricot on the horizon and an apricot in the sky. The water is flat. It's just so flat. And I'm the child. I'm the breath of fresh air. I'm the looping arc of birds and art. I am your programme. I am my programme. I am all our names in small font at the end of the movie. I am your mouth around a crisp, finishing, a crunch.

THE BODY IS MADE OF PEOPLE AND TRUTH

'There must be a kiln inside everyone
that holds up the body
that wants to return to mud'

— Kim Hyesoon, 'To Bake a Star', translated by Don Mee Choi, p. 11

The truth

The truth they say is in the trees. In the roots. In the leaves. The truth comes and goes. The truth is. The truth was. The Truth. You knew before we knew before they knew before she knew. We knew not very much because we couldn't acknowledge anything. The fire. The sky. The trees they were all together. And then they were really together. And then the smoke was thicker than everything else. We could have drawn our own attention. We could have laid down runway lighting. We could have made music and songs and signs of the times of everything of the whole entire place we could have. And what was it keeping us from doing that? Who were the voices the places the rules that kept us singing smaller songs and telling tinier tales. Let us take you out to the lake. Let us show you the scores in the earth. Let us find the way you remember the way you forget the way we all ignore it all. Take your hands and put them in ours. Let us hold our bodies in close proximity. Let us be of each other. Let it all fall in line. We thought desire could keep us occupied at least long enough to get through it all. But it didn't make a dent in it. Didn't touch the sides. Desire dies in the face of all this. We lay together. We lay together. We just lay together and that was it. Under the trees that soon caught fire and we had to retreat. We were retreating when it went a little further into darkness and the desire left us. The desire had already gone. The desire was wandering in the night looking for a new host. A new way of being. We could have told you about this earlier. They could have told us about this earlier. We all could have been properly and clearly informed at a time where we could have still done something but it wouldn't have mattered. The choices were made. The decisions were fumbled. The time drained through the hourglass at the regular pace. The brain is only capable of handling so much and we have exceeded the complexity we are capable of. It's not a number. It's not a series of interactions. It's not a state machine diagram moving off into infinity. No large language model will save us, even if it has a cute name. We are here together with just our naked bodies to save us and we remain unsaved. We remain.

The tilt

Just the sound of laughter. The first time I realised I could see through you and into me. Make a sound as you let yourself drop. I see you covered in dust, covered in dirt. This is the cold feeling that rolls through like surf. I take it. I take it and let the air feel fuller around me because of you. Down the street I say the faces tilt at you and you say the faces tilt at me. The faces tilt in all directions. Then none. We are watching faces on sticks like you can follow the sun, follow the moon, follow me home. In this house your hands on my body are like passwords. I say nothing and the sound grows louder. I say more and the room is too loud to be in together. Both your hands on my jaw and I shatter. It is not like the experience would suggest. It is not like anything else. I feel you through cotton worn thin. I know what this looks like. I know the exact feeling of your pulse under my thumb, which should not be used to measure it. The voice that tells me things says that I can trust you. Several other voices would usually disagree but they are quiet when you're in here. We know to be a person is to be multiple people crowding a footpath. I know almost nothing, for the thousandth time. You slip your hand up my thigh seeking your god, my god, the head of everything, the godhead. Tell me about your spirit in the form of a child lost in a department store, the speakers echoing your name, echoing your name. I draw myself up into the towering representation of self I create from moment to moment. It is the Buddha-sized cabbage I saw on the internet and longed for immediately, its white base, its flat green leaves. Imagine me as a brassica. Imagine me cruciferous. Just spend some time thinking about me. It's how I know it's real. Tilt your face toward me. I am the sky as an imperative. I heard you as the sound of the day closing in. I heard you as the sound of this plate breaking in my hands. We say we don't hurt each other only to hurt each other with the pieces of real life. I used to always feel the hand drawn back for a blow. I was trained for it. I feel your pulse again with a thumb. This is to feel two pulses and confuse them for one. I confuse it all for one.

The body house the house of the body

In this house the entranceway is soft like you're a teenager walking through a muffled, carpeted, newly built suburban house. It's thick with wool and silence. A house full of Yankee Candles, a pandemic peak measuring tool in this age. It is so quiet in here. The socks reach my knees and the silence collects around the soles of my feet muffling up toward my legs like corridors leading through and up into the central vaunted ceilings of my belly. You're telling me a cis teen built this chapel? If only this stomach was a place of quiet worship and contemplation. Its skin like white stained glass, ripples dissecting light, the great hollow centre of the earth you shout and it echoes back around to find my neck following the vagus nerve like breadcrumbs back home you hope to see me but you're inside me looking out over a landscape that ripples like stones and riverbeds and mountain ranges or hills. These eyes don't see at present. They're the domed skylights of my childhood sitting in a roof or a wall or something unseeing but seen. You see my fingers in the dusk, splayed out as a deck for stargazing or looking across the tussock land we're lying on. What is a body from the inside out. What is a house but a body made bigger. What is it to say that here I am with my muscled back as a base for you. My spine the path you follow the path I follow to find home. Here in the base of my skull is a bed for you in the mushroom nest of my lobes. Eyelids like blinds. My blood the white noise you crave for sleep. My heart the tick-tock of a non-existent clock. This house is not a house. It is a home.

The rain in twenty years

It is raining twenty years from now. The clouds break and then restore themselves over and over again. Sunshine a pause between showers. It is raining in twenty years when the earth still continues, and the thunder and lightning still crackle and roll over the December heat. Twenty years back and forward and back again. I carry a bowl of pudding through the rain, somewhere. I whip cream in humidity, somehow. The memories of a you I hadn't met yet. Or the you I've spent almost twenty years with. Or the you I don't even know still exists, please exist. This is all hope and a fever dream. This is all distorted by my brain in neutral. These are all the things I realise far too late. The brain hates itself. It makes trouble even from a neutral state. It is trouble in all states. It is only mistakes. Spending time forward or back but not here. Spending time like it is nothing, worth very little, everywhere. Spending it with a reckless heart. Spending. The rain in twenty years is ceaseless and the streets flood. The rain in twenty years is never enough and always too much. Both and neither like some big joke where we're the central theme and it's all our fault. I grow my hair. I return to trousers. I watch my skin settle and line and fade. My hands become my grandmother's and my mother's in turn depending on the way you look. I look like my mother when she was forty. I look like genes folded in two and in two again, cut to shape and concertinaed like paper dolls. I stretch myself across a doorway, a mantel, an archway looking back through these paper selves holding hands and holding hands. In twenty years, paper might be a miracle. In twenty years, it's raining

I am

For Always

I am an unmade bed. I am a single thing made up of many other things. I am a reason, a raising, a roof to be raised. I am a song you sing in your sleep. I am a collection of dots. I am a need you buried in the back garden. I am a literal spray of light across a wooden floor in a house where the sun has only just returned. I am a musical phrase. I am a lead light. I am a host. I am seven different names. I am all the fat in my body. I am the sky when it is early spring and I can't believe I exist in this colour range. I am so blue. I am so blue. I am just waiting in an eternal place where I am endlessly questioning time and then it's a decade later and I am not a wrinkle, I am not an age. I am the same hyperbole and underestimation I use to throw things into relief. I am a build-up of power in a body. I am a rest period between sets of other things. I am a sheet, spread beneath us. I am a night where I follow the moon and your mouth around the city. I am a pure clear rush of anger that burns out all other feelings from my body. I am a hollow. I am a gully. I am a valley. I am a riverbed. I am a beech forest. I am a canyon worn by water. I am the five million years it took. I am several different dogs, of the same breed, across several different continents. I am a woollen sweater, knitted by hand across an entire winter. I am a letter, a lover, a list. I am a line of muscle in a body. I am a hamstring. I am an Achilles. I am an ankle. I am a dripping tap in a kitchen. I am a hand curling around a neck. I am a neck with fingers winding around it. I am milk. I am money. I am a house you built yourself. I am a speech. I am a goodbye. I am a broken wrist. I am a bone healed correctly. I am the rugby league concussion test. I am a series of strong drinks. I am an unsynchronised manual transmission. I am a driver capable of a double declutch. I am a neutral tone. I am an A string. I am always the high E on the A string of a cello. I am the shearling coat you're wearing. I am a scent you put on for me. I am an origami butterfly you fold for me. I am your open, empty hands.

We are

We are something. We are something together. We are a space a race a race condition a tiny little signal sent between stars between lobes between neurons between here and home. Between there and home. Between. The stars are not enough for us. The race the pace the night continues and we are something we are nothing we are over it all together and never together at all. This is not nothing. This is only something if it's only nothing later. The arms of the sky. The weak grip of the newly awakened heart. The way that it all just sounds off and sounds off and then all sound is gone it is off it is never. We would never have known any difference any thing anything else. *Thus Spake Zarathustra*. Our bodies. Every body. This thin slice of thin slices of thinness of the unholy yet godly obsession with nothing. We were to not exist except we exist and should apologise for all existence as we exist. There was a special place and a special posture and a special man to say this to. There is a little house to enter and never leave. There are hearts upon hearts and we all know the names and the words and the order of recitation. We direct our faces to this sky to this person to this idea of three things as one thing as three things as one. It is as ridiculous as it sounds and the sound of it is breath simply escaping from a mouth we once admired and no longer do. We were once admired. We no longer do anything. We are admired, underadmired, admired exactly as we deserve and we receive all the fingers that are due to us or we don't ever do anything real or feel anything at all. We three, we four, we five. We two. We are clearly up for discussion. We are clearly just the start of it. We are clearly and wholly indecipherable which we're told is as we should be. We never knew where the start was and that was useful information to have. We are what you would expect of the underinformed, the type of people we are. The good at heart the faint of heart the lionhearted the simple and sweet the you know we know they know no one really knows anything. That is all it was all it ever will be. We're still as nothing as we started. We know.

Apple skins

I dream an earthquake or I think I do later truth shaves it back to memory
then the memory of remembering the difference makes one body my body
feel like two different bodies then I'm next to your body and his body and
everybody is many bodies and it's a very short time to being bodies on
bodies on bodies on bodies   the sudden interruption is
also a memory and this time it's the memory of the softest mouth in the
world holding me in nothing less than rapture for the briefest of moments
            the next interruption is the time it takes to think about thinking
about thinking about the moment we're pared back to nothing together in
a place where our slowly revealing apple skins are shed in rings in snakes
in coils we are around ourselves and each other and there's no edge to our
edges it's all the same   I might have seen into the future
when I was sent out of my body by your kiss but I might have also just seen
into myself from ten thousand perspectives at once and it's so hard to say
which is which when you're dizzied and breathing like you're inside out
when you're inside out from the discovery of an entirely new truth that is
cracking through you at speed and in heat and you are helped down steps
and wander into an evening   awake

If only

If only if only. I could have used my mouth to transmit some meaning. I could have left or come home or done some sort of in between combo of any of these. I could have been the bulldozer, the demolition team, the engineer who respectfully tells you your house is falling down. I could have been the termite expert. I could have diagnosed myself in every single discipline from cardiology to neurology. I could have looked into the back of my eyeballs to see the film playing upside down in there. I could have dug the grave myself. I just chose not to. In the grand tradition of ostriches I declined every avenue but continuation on the same trajectory. I checked out every library book and stacked them in the spare room. I ignored every email about the fines until they sent me a letter. But even then I only read it. I didn't pick up a single call. Didn't even listen to the voice messages. Might as well have spent five years in a hut in the Antarctic. I shut the curtains to my own eyes and stuffed things deep inside my heart. I turned to goo inside a cocoon. I fermented slowly in a jar in the fridge. I hibernated in a burrow deep underground. I just survived. I just survived like a sea monkey, like a seed shat out by megafauna, like the mould in your bathroom. Clinging to it. Limpets. Every type of life. The unknown uncoloured fluff in your umbilicus. Your eyelid mites. The spring bulbs you buried. The cock-a-roaches. The way that the varicella-zoster virus lives on inside you to become shingles, years post chicken pox. I survived like the astronauts in the ISS, with many weird modifications to what you'd consider a normal life. That one ex you just fucking see everywhere, all the time, forever. Like the bacteria varieties that live in hot water or weird sediment or the Mariana Trench. The office plants that despite receiving no care, attention or light just continue to cling to the realm of living. Your ninety-year-old grandfather who frankly just looks like wax paper stretched over skin. The oldest golden retriever in the world who is twenty years old and whose face is entirely white. Weeds. Like weeds. I survived like old man's beard and any invasive species. The koi that overtake streams. I swam. I was a list of actions repeated. Kept in after school I wrote lines and lines. It will not always be like this. It will not always be like

The bed made of bodies

I lie awake in bed beside a body imagining other bodies touching me. I see us side to side with our arms entangled and our breath commingling. I roll over and other bodies are there. More bodies. Legs and crook of an arm the hook of an elbow the twist of an ankle the slope of a waist. There are no voices. Only the sound of skin or the click of a swallow. More bodies arrive. They are put to work against each other. A jigsaw that's sweating now. A carpet of people lying closely together as they breathe. They have to breathe, obviously. Their lungs fill without them and with them. The night grows lighter with all these hands together, resting. Occasionally there is a sigh and a gentle murmur to comfort follows. Some bodies drop into a deeper breathing that suggests sleep. Others turn to face another. This is still not enough comfort. I still somehow crave to be held more deeply. Someone strokes my hair. A hand rests on my thigh, my hip, my cheek. I cried myself to sleep alone as an infant. I cry myself to sleep with company in my imagination. With bodies and bodies around me my eyes puff and my skin reddens. I sniff. My body shakes and the bodies around me are shaken or shaking. Eventually we are all crying in my imagination. The biggest bed in the world made of bodies and comfort. Made of crying and breathing. We could cry forever. We could make the bed an ocean. We could be the ocean rising up to meet ourselves as translucent green water. We do turn into the ocean and this time I'm a jellyfish and all the bodies are other jellyfish and somehow we're all pressed together as one. In the daylight we wake to forget we're all pressed together as one though we're still all pressed together as one. I remember in the dawn when for a moment we were pressed together as

Giantess

I step into another body. It's a bigger body. A shell. I echo in it. I rattle in it. Then it snaps to fit. And now I'm this larger person. This performance will be louder for the simple fact of my biology, my new biology. I always wanted to be larger, taller, longer. I want to reach things, so many things. I wanted to take up a lot more space than was given to me. I wanted to step over fences and see further into the city. I wanted to be able to cradle you in the crook of my arm. I wanted to be free from all the compromises of this body, not large enough but still too large. In this vision I am now capable of so many more things. Small children still look up into me like I'm the newest thing they've seen today. Their eyes widen at the sight of me. They don't have the ability to understand this and yet they understand me. I think the plaintive call of tantrums pulls us closer. I wish to lie on the floor and drag my arms and legs around. I want to be left alone or to be offered snacks or to be kept company while the energy travels through my body and out into the world. Adults forget. I am pulled back by the size of me to this place of overwhelming feeling. It has no way to exit me. The feelings on the internal racetrack of my bones. My big bones. My really big bones. They amplify the noise of the racetrack so that I am buzzed by my own feelings. I am a giantess and nothing can hold me back from making the earth shake. The earth shakes and shakes and I am a one step a two step a pattern of feet and music. I am your creation. I exist in skin that should be mine.

One metre

Each human is one metre apart in an arrangement we were not used to before this perfect vision. Each piece of you is received as something not unlike a gift. I've heard voices talking out in the hallway and understood nothing. Then I've stood across from you only able to lip read my way through to you. It is a gentle dimming of possibility like lights through a long-distance journey at night. It is as I thought all along: we are both threats and promises. Do you know that both can be contained and restrained by the right words, by the right spelling? And both are visible even at night. You say that you say that you say. A cough hidden in a throat clearing. It's a good game to be small and to hide. An even better game is to be large and free. The best game is to see the same question in the faces of others: what are you? Never answering I just continue. I am the breeze. I have been the light, the trees and the night. I am just cells layered up like lacquer, like resin, like subcutaneous fat. You don't need to know what I am. You don't need to see anything other than what you're already looking at. You don't know what you're looking at. I am what you're looking at.

Womb at night

I was the eyes, the ears, the nose of the place. Look at me as I transition through the loops, the hoops left for me like signals, like glasses, like the signs you see to make things better. The rhythm of this night. You said you dreaded me. You said you could never quite lift up to the horizon. What's dead in me now. What's dread in you later. What's the surprise. What's the question. What's the life inside of all of us. I was carried inside my grandmother as an egg. A small round of rude health ready to go thirty-three years later. Do you know what you'll say in the moment you're inside a womb inside another womb. The voice of the littlest lamb left laughing. I am a cascade of night. I am the courtly concept of love. I was. I am. I will be. This night is a blip on the horizon where my body reeks of pain and hardship. Where I bleed from a room I was supposed to house someone in. You can house everyone in the right cityscape. You can house the sky in your eyes with the right level of attention. This woman keeps looking at this man like he is made out of something more valuable than I can see. Tonight there's a sharpness that won't go to bed. In this night there's the sound you made when your mother tucked you in. In this night you tell me nothing on top of something. The air holds the sweet scent of my grandmother. The talcum powder gist of her. The valleys of her wrinkled hands. The night can do as much as a womb can.

The human body

The body comes as a surprise to no one. It is soft and pliable. It is completely and utterly smooth. It is you, and you. Over time things change. The body is interpreted differently by different brains with different requirements. Softness is actually a pleasure, actually. Though, at times, they tell you it's a big fucking problem. But then there's the fleshy tensing of muscles underneath. And unbelievably the reaction is the same. It's a liability love, I don't know what to tell you. The body strains to make itself the right shape. The body grows and depletes. It changes, re-sorts itself into different sets, different suits. The skin, still soft, but now empty in places and full in others, striped like pyjamas and tigers. The body grips itself at the hips. The fleshy intensity of it. The way it's five handfuls of itself. The (grudging) deliciousness of it all. All human bodies are the same in equal parts. No one wants to look yet everyone wants to look. Everyone especially wants to touch. A touch to the small of the back. A request to go under the bra. A hand on a thigh. An entire fake-out routine to touch one side of one tit. 'You are the most attractive fat body I've ever met.' 'You are the softest centre of the earth.' Only until you're not. And you're not. The body resembles the cottage cheese they lied about. The body returns to the foods they tried to torture it with. The body has its own opinions it keeps to itself. It writes musical notation or a discrete set of numbers it will likely refuse to show you. The body has its own drum, its own marching band and its own baton. And so it marches.

The wrong stories

I know why. The lines in me run along possibilities. I am visible. I am invisible. I am nothing. I am everything. To switch between the expanse of nothing and the expanse of everything is disorienting. I pull the energy of the universe into me and wrap it around like a shelter. Then I'm not even a particle. What have you told me about myself that I still retain, stuck under the skin like a pebble in a graze. There are some things you just cannot communicate about. I can't communicate when you don't hear me. Trapped under glass like a beetle tapping on the side with my mandibles, my jawbone. Your balloon. I deflate. You tell stories about me, in front of me, without me. The stories are wrong. They are also the wrong stories. The stories are stories about you but with me in them. I'm in them because we're together, here. But I'm just an audience. That's the cruellest part of me. But it's your show. I'm just attempting to exist through this. I am rolling with the punches. A problem of endurance is enduring. Digging upwards for air to find the way out. Tumbled by a wave. Stuck in the bedding. Unable to get the clothing over my head. Where do my arms come out of this garment? What time is it? I am following the white rabbit that I most recently glimpsed but its ancestors are the ones I remember deep within me. They've worn such well-trodden paths with their little feet. It's always those fucking bunnies I'm following down into a place I will just have to leave again. But I leave again. I leave again. I remember so much more at the surface. I remember that they are the wrong stories, the wrong rabbits, it's the wrong path. I turn around.

Don't touch me

I find myself hovering over the days. They come and they go. Then they go and are gone again. I am stuck to the road like discarded gum. Unable to stretch and stand for myself. I elide like a French sentence. I run myself together like a link of shopping carts. I work to turn the corner like I'm spreading out into eternity, past the edges of the known universe. I no longer know what is exactly true and at some point I think I knew, I really think I did. I have spent a long time walking a thin line alongside someone else. Not quite touching. These days I'm usually of the no-touching polarity. I have gone back and forth over this life. Touch me or don't. I set the rules and reject all-comers. In this sludge state I know two things to be true. Don't touch me and don't touch me. The sadness becomes just such a tiredness. A base layer like crushed rock beneath pavers. I am my own crushed rock made of a tiredness built from sadness built from all these things that have simply just happened. I crushed this rock with mine own hands. I built this layer of foundation with the sheer force of my will. I have been here for so long now it is a privilege to be alive and I hold that close to my heart. I have over time become more and more. I have over time narrowed down. I have straightened up. I have curved with a purpose known only to time and myself. Sometimes only to time. I can slip this small wish into my own fortune, behind my own back. I can do all these things I said I could do. I can do them all. And perhaps I might even do them. I have layered the foundations. I have checked the timetable. I have looked at the moon to see the phase, to see the trajectory. I have bought the pavers. I have sown the seed. I have turned on the grow lights. I have engaged the first gear. I have let the clutch out slowly enough, just enough. I have felt the bath draw through the darkness. I have turned this cold night into a different night, six months later. I have transmogrified everything that was open to me. And here I stand as sad as ever but still lifting each foot as the time comes for it to be lifted. The feet tell you. They know. They migrate like caribou. Seeking and seeking. And seeking. I have been from A to B. I have been here and there. I am still seeking myself. I have sought others but now I am only able to search for myself. To search for myself. The purest cause. The coldest night. The darkest moon. The lowest light. When will this fucking thing end.

When will it. Only who knows. Who is it that knows and do I know them? Who will tell me? When will I know? When? I know enough about knowing to know I know nothing. But it is not enough. It has never been enough. You have to tell me. Do you know?

Heavy men

I forget that men are heavy. Their bodies and bones on top of me feel different. Their muscles are large, their limbs just bigger and their eyes will still reveal some kind of drowning in something if you have been sitting in their laps correctly. I have been sitting in their laps correctly. On the same night a man convinces me to fuck him in a hotel room another man jokes about my lack of attractiveness in the wide open and full dark street. He does it in front of his friend who was looking into me, perhaps seeing how recently I had been fucked. Possibly not thinking what his friend was thinking. I walk on ignoring them. Men like this, masculinity like this. The rest of us always sliced up into the wafer-thin entries in the fuckability stakes, a tissue paper pink slip. In any moment I could get fucked by any number of men. Liking any of them is the real stretch. And you, on this street, say I am low value. And you, on this street, drunk and getting drunker. In rooms recently there have been too many men. Too little of me. It always has to be noticed and then explained. Please don't say eye-candy. Please don't refer to any part of my body as anything ever. Please don't say my name like that. Please remember, I'm not a woman. Just always someone somehow begging to be treated like a single human. Just as if I was someone worthy of the most basic decency. Here I am asking people who haven't thought for a moment about anything to treat me with care and attention. The results are always the same. The luxury of ignorance, the casual cruelty, the long-term disposability of all perceived low-value bodies and genders. This body, though low value to you, is the body I am contained in and the least you could do is refrain from revealing your punchable face in the street. The rest of us have to look at you and the despair is too heavy to carry in these times. The despair drags me to the ground when you care so much about nothing that matters very much. The despair somehow doesn't touch you in your large castle. Safe inside a fortress. Safe inside the cultural connotations of domination. The rest of us live where we live. In the frequent unsafety of your disapproval. It started when I first talked back to my father. The first man.

The marriage pact

She will tell you it all. With her mouth a little ajar, a little agog. The teeth of these white men lead their bodies into view. They know how they command a room and it would be boring if it wasn't also the way things are. It's still boring. No one here knows your name, let's be honest. It's all just a bit of a thing, a little way of saying what you know without knowing what you say. Her mouth, she lets it fall closed. It is all smooth, like a shark. The men. The men. But when you touch their obliques it can all fall away for a minute. The feeling of muscle moving under skin like a shot in the heart. For a moment. And then, and yet, and then. The circling gyre of hot air lifting it all up into the heavens where you'd believe they belong if you didn't look too closely. All out of sight out of mind out of time. I am a completely different dimension to these fucks. But somehow still I want them. If only this was an urge that could be scooped out. I'm the inside of an egg, freeing myself from myself. Free me, free to you, free us all later. A man tells me a mother-in-law joke and insists it means nothing about hating women despite being part of a long narrative drive towards hating women. Men as ranks closing. Men as a tacit agreement to not break the line. Still writing about men. Still doing it. Because they still require confrontation. And I tend towards it. I tend towards confusing and upsetting. I tend towards it. Leaning like trees living in a wind. I do.

Heal thyself

We witnessed an exchange of sorts. An exchange in each other. A leaving, a returning, some kind of thing where it seemed like we both made out equally but one of us definitely got the better end of the deal than the other. But maybe that is just the way it looks from one angle. Hard to say when you can really only see things from one side. I tried to tell a story that included more perspectives, but I found I was limited by my own imagination which is to say there's a certain lack of facts that can't really be worked around. There's a way, there's a way, there's a way until there's not. Fast forward and what's the capability of change. What's the level of lying to yourself that's tenable in a decade-long period. Is it lying to yourself if you just don't know the truth? There's no truth. There was a type of truth. Truth is subjective and heavily medicated at all times. You would have me believe so many different things I simply wouldn't know myself at all. I've tried to know myself, know thyself. Heal thyself. Etc. Thinking about the self too much is its own kind of poison. Its own lack of reward. Its own trap. We paste ourselves into other spaces and say nothing about it. I will say nothing about it. The ghosts of Christmases past still entertain me. At the bar they order drinks that fall through their absent bodies to the floor. You have to care to be in on it. You have to care to be out of it. You have to care entirely too much to be not tugged ruthlessly into the atmosphere. Later, I will regret caring as much as I have for as long as I have. I will regret even more than that later. But for now, I drink this drink without you.

Shake the tree

She shakes the tree for the rain of fruit. She shakes the tree for the feeling of fullness, relief, pause from the work of everything else. She shakes the tree like the earth is impatient for love, for more. And in shaking the tree she is lost, removed, welcomed to a home she never knew. You can or cannot return to your roots. You can be descended from orchardists and understand why apple trees make you ache. You can live alone in a room by yourself thinking only about the touch of others. You can do whatever seems most possible at the time. Or whatever seems most impossible. There are two streets facing off in a T-junction and these are all your choices. What are the rules of turning? Are you giving way? Any of us could give way at any moment. The gentle lowering of a head to signal something, anything. You could be a child who has run away. You could be a person relaxing into the relief of a new love. You could be another such thing in a list. Or you could be none of them. One of them. Some of them. What could you be. She shakes the tree for the blizzard of leaves, for the rain of blossom, for the yet to be.

Acknowledgements

The most important thank you for any Pākehā writer is to mihi to all mana whenua of Aotearoa for their generosity in the face of continued acts of non-consent and disrespect by us, their treaty partners. I am truly privileged to be a treaty partner, to have this place to stand, and to receive repeated gifts and offerings of manaakitanga. These started in my very early years in Ōtautahi and continue in my life now in Te Whanganui-a-Tara. There cannot be thanks or koha enough, only work to lead to a true and real partnership that lives up to Te Tiriti. I said this same thing in my last book, and it is even more important now, in these times. I am here by virtue of Te Tiriti and I do not take that for granted. Toitū te Tiriti!

Thank you to my readers. The best part of releasing books is hearing from readers. Every Instagram story, email, and passed-on thank you for *I Am in Bed with You* or Show Ponies was a delight.

I wrote this book perched at the end of the bar at Golding's Free Dive in Te Aro. Thank you to Golding's and its staff and patrons for letting me be an energy vampire in the corner.

Thank you to my first readers who provided valuable feedback on the first draft of this book: Sarah Jane Barnett, Always Becominging, Liz Breslin, Christine Brooks and Khye. Thank you to Sugar Magnolia Wilson and Hannah Mettner for early feedback on some of these poems. Thank you to the AUP team: Sam Elworthy, Lauren Donald, Katharina Bauer, Sophia Broom, Emma Neale, Kalee Jackson and Emily Goldthorpe, and many more behind the scenes. I remain astounded by the effort and energy that goes into one single book, let alone the many released each year. Thank you for your care and attention.

Thank you to Freya Daly Sadgrove for Show Ponies. What a magical experience you create over and over and over. Thank you to Christine Brooks, Uther Dean, Jean Sergent and Olivia Hall for being my excellent chorus. Thank you to Chris Tse for your many generosities. Thank you to

Paula Green for all your work. Thank you to all my visible and invisible cheerleaders. Thank you to all the poets.

It is always through connection with people I find myself coming back to writing again and again. Without everyone and the feelings I have about you all I doubt I'd ever write anything. I'm sorry I can't thank you all by name. I think you know how much you mean to me! Thank you to Sarah Jane Barnett for repairs, conversation and errands. Thank you to Always Becominging for always becoming and so many things. Thank you to Juniper Bevensee for knives, axes and conversation. Thank you to Sugar Magnolia Wilson for being there for my specific book-related feelings and many other feelings. Thank you to The Beloved Chicken Pot Pies. Thank you to Siân and Creek for encouragement, love and excitement. Thank you to Craig Spence and Kenese Lautusi for all the dinners and laughs. Thank you to Helen Rickerby for our many extended conversations. Thank you to Tria Manley for knowing me for so long and still getting to know me. Thank you to Stevie Wilder for all the memes and cute conversations. Thank you to Bryn Oakly for keeping in touch. Thank you to all past, present and future acquaintances, lovers and friends.

Thank you to my family.

Thank you, as always, to my beloved Simon Carryer. It's been twenty-one years and I wouldn't want to do this life with anyone else even though it has recently contained: a pandemic, multiple redundancies, health issues, deaths, and all the other challenges alongside the many thousands of little joys. Thank you for building with me. Thank you again and still for all the breakfasts in bed. Thank you for loving the goblin.

The epigraphs in this book are all from people I consider my literary ancestors. I have drawn comfort and knowledge from their works over my adult life. As a writer I am descended from every author I've read and loved. These are a small selection of some of the more impactful ones, ones that help me make sense to all my selves.

Previously Published and References

'If only' was previously published in *The Spinoff* Friday Poem, September 2020.

The epigraphs are taken from the following editions and reproduced with permission:

Carson, Anne, *An Oresteia*, Farrar, Straus and Giroux, 2009.

Kim, Hyesoon, *All of the Garbage of the World, Unite!*, translated by Don Mee Choi, Action Books, 2001.

Le Guin, Ursula K.,*The Lathe of Heaven*, Scribner, 2008.

Nin, Anaïs, *Seduction of the Minotaur*, Swallow Press, 1961.

EMMA BARNES (Pākehā, they/them) studied at the University of Canterbury and lives in Aro Valley, Te Whanganui-a-Tara, Wellington. Their poetry has been published in journals including *Landfall*, *Turbine | Kapohau*, *Cordite* and *Best New Zealand Poems* (2008, 2010, 2021). They performed in *Show Ponies* in 2022 and 2023. They are the author of the poetry collection *I Am in Bed with You* (AUP, 2021) and co-editor with Chris Tse of *Out Here: An Anthology of Takatāpui and LGBTQIA+ Writers from Aotearoa* (AUP, 2021). They work in tech and spend a lot of time picking up heavy things and putting them back down again.